FIELD TRIPS

AQUARIUMS

Kathleen Reitmann and Heather Kissock

AV2

www.av2books.com

Step 1
Go to www.av2books.com

Step 2
Enter this unique code

RWHLS4TY5

Step 3
Explore your interactive eBook!

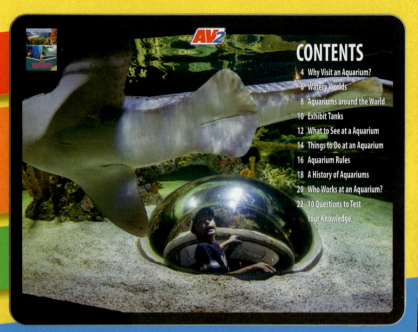

AV2 is optimized for use on any device

Your interactive eBook comes with...

Contents
Browse a live contents page to easily navigate through resources

Audio
Listen to sections of the book read aloud

Videos
Watch informative video clips

Weblinks
Gain additional information for research

Try This!
Complete activities and hands-on experiments

Key Words
Study vocabulary, and complete a matching word activity

Quizzes
Test your knowledge

Slideshows
View images and captions

--- ... and much, much more! ---

View new titles and product videos at www.av2books.com

FIELD TRIPS
AQUARIUMS

Contents

- 2   AV2 Book Code
- 4   Why Visit an Aquarium?
- 6   Watery Worlds
- 8   Aquariums around the World
- 10 Exhibit Tanks
- 12 What to See at an Aquarium
- 14 Things to Do at an Aquarium
- 16 Aquarium Rules
- 18 A History of Aquariums
- 20 Who Works at an Aquarium?
- 22 10 Questions to Test Your Knowledge
- 23 Key Word/Index

Aquariums   3

Why Visit an Aquarium?

Aquariums give people the chance to learn about **aquatic** life. Visitors can view aquatic creatures from all over the world here. They can watch these animals and learn more about their behavior.

A visit to an aquarium can also help visitors understand the importance of the world's oceans, lakes, and rivers. People can see how animals need these waters to survive. They can also learn about how these **habitats** are in danger.

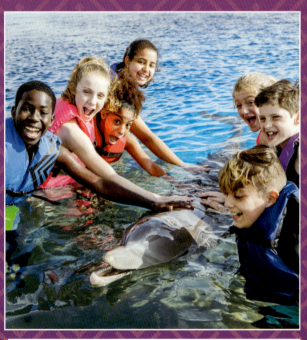

Field trips to aquariums can sometimes include special access to the facility's residents, such as dolphins.

Watery Worlds

All aquariums house aquatic life. Some aquariums specialize in certain types of animals. An **oceanarium** only houses saltwater animals. A dolphinarium focuses solely on dolphins.

Aquariums serve different purposes. Some are meant for public access. People are welcome to come and visit. Others are more private in nature and are open only to scientists and researchers.

Public Aquariums

A public aquarium is a type of zoo. Instead of land animals, however, it focuses on aquatic life. The animals are kept in large water tanks. They are there for people to see.

Research Aquariums

These aquariums give scientists the opportunity to learn more about aquatic animals. The animals kept here are studied for research purposes. Scientists analyze their behavior and compare different **species**.

Conservation Aquariums

Conservation aquariums house aquatic animals in need of rescue. Many of the animals found here are at risk of going **extinct**. Others may be injured and are being nursed back to health.

Marine Parks

A **marine** park keeps marine life for entertainment purposes. The sea animals found here, such as dolphins and orcas, are trained to perform for large audiences. These aquariums are often found at theme parks.

Aquariums around the World

Aquariums are found in countries around the world. They are popular attractions for both locals and tourists alike.

1
Georgia Aquarium
Atlanta, United States

The Georgia Aquarium is the largest aquarium in the United States. More than 10,000 animals are housed in the aquarium's 10 million gallons (37.9 million liters) of water.

2
AquaRio
Rio de Janeiro, Brazil

At South America's largest aquarium, visitors can see 5,000 animals in 28 tanks. The aquarium's Oceanic Enclosure features a tunnel. People can walk through it while sharks and rays swim overhead.

Field Trips

3
Moscow Oceanarium
Moscow, Russia

One of Europe's largest aquariums, the Moscow Oceanarium features marine life from all over the world. Animals ranging from octopuses to orcas can be found in its 6.6 million gallons (25 million L) of water.

4
uShaka Marine World
Durban, South Africa

This aquarium is found within the uShaka Marine World theme park. Its 32 tanks contain more than 10,000 marine species. The aquarium allows visitors to snorkel in its fish lagoon and dive with sharks.

5
Shanghai Ocean Aquarium
Shanghai, China

This aquarium is home to the world's longest **submarine** viewing tunnel, at 170 yards (155 meters). The aquarium is separated into zones. Each features a different aquatic environment.

6
SEA LIFE Sydney Aquarium
Sydney, Australia

SEA LIFE Sydney Aquarium houses aquatic life **native** to Australia's waters. The aquarium is home to more than 13,000 animals. Visitors can watch creatures such as stingrays and dugongs in action.

Aquariums 9

Viewing Area
At least one part of the tank will have a viewing area. Glass and **acrylic** are the most common materials used for this area. They are safe for most creatures, and people can see clearly through them.

Aquascaping
Most tanks try to re-create the natural habitat of the aquatic life living there. The animals can swim through rock formations and dine on the plants found inside the tank.

Signage
Most tanks have signs near the viewing area. The signs feature facts about the animals in the tank. They name the animals, and supply information on their size, diet, and habitat.

Exhibit Tanks

Aquariums have large **exhibit** tanks for their animals. The water in these tanks is similar to the water found in the animals' natural habitats. Animals that share the same natural habitat are often grouped together in the same tank.

The tanks must be kept safe for the animals inside. The walls of the tank, including the viewing area, must be strong enough to hold the animals and the water they need to survive. Some tanks may not need much water. The size and number of animals in the tank determines the amount of water needed.

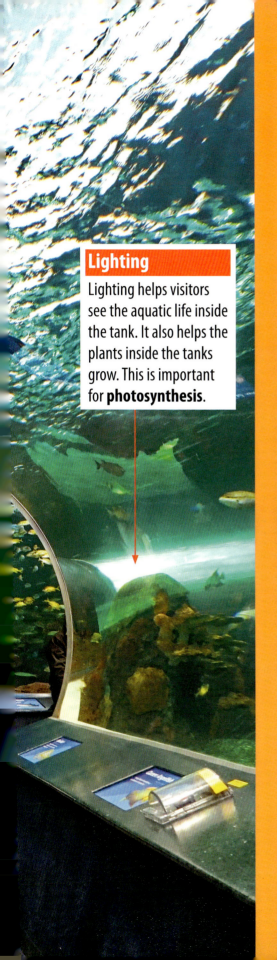

Lighting
Lighting helps visitors see the aquatic life inside the tank. It also helps the plants inside the tanks grow. This is important for **photosynthesis**.

Some aquarium tanks feature domes that come up into the exhibit. These domes allow guests to immerse themselves in the activity happening around them.

Aquariums 11

What to See at an Aquarium

Besides showcasing aquatic life, many aquariums also participate in programs that help both people and animals. Some of these programs explore the challenges facing these animals in nature and what can be done to help them. Other programs focus on how aquatic life can assist in treating human diseases.

Mote Marine Laboratory and Aquarium

This research aquarium in Sarasota, Florida, focuses much of its work on the conservation of marine resources. Visitors are able to view the Mote **laboratories**. Here, they can watch scientists at work and learn more about their research studies.

Aquarium of the Pacific

Visitors to this aquarium in Long Beach, California, should be sure to see its exhibit of corals and sponges. The aquarium is working with medical scientists to see how these two marine **organisms** can be used to fight cancer and other human diseases.

National Aquarium

The National Aquarium's Animal Care and Rescue Center is located in Baltimore, Maryland. Here, aquarium staff care for rescued animals. During a building tour, guests can talk to staff and watch them in action, participate in hands-on activities, including a mock fish surgery, and learn more about the aquarium's operations.

SEA LIFE Michigan Aquarium

A visit to Auburn Hill's SEA LIFE Michigan Aquarium would not be complete without seeing Benson and Carr. These two green sea turtles were rescued after being injured by boat propellers. The aquarium works with turtle rescue groups around the world to find homes for turtles that can no longer survive in the ocean.

The **Aquarium of the Pacific** is home to more than **11,000 animals**.

The **National Aquarium** hosts more than **1.3 million visitors** every year.

A **green sea turtle** can **hold its breath** under water for **up to 7 hours**.

Aquariums 13

Tours often include talks on the anatomy of the animals found at the aquarium. Guides use models to show important body parts.

Things to Do at an Aquarium

Most aquariums provide visitors with the chance to explore aquatic life in detail. Many aquariums hold tours. During the tour, a guide points out important features of the animals and their natural habitats. Some aquariums offer classes and camps. Going to a camp allows people to spend days learning about the animals.

Aquariums often hold events throughout the day as well. Visitors can see animals being fed. They can watch animal training sessions. Some aquariums even let people help out behind the scenes.

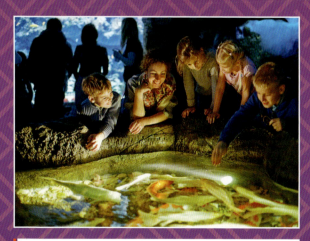

Touch tanks are popular exhibits at aquariums, offering visitors a hands-on experience with aquatic life.

Aquarium Rules

It is important that both animals and people enjoy their time at the aquarium. This is why aquariums set rules for people to follow. Animals and staff should always be respected.

6 Simple Rules

1. Never tap or bang on tanks and displays. This can scare the animals.

2. Do not feed or touch animals unless you have permission from aquarium staff. Some animals may be on special diets.

3. Do not run through the aquarium. Someone could get hurt.

4. Listen carefully to your guide and do as he or she says. This will keep both you and the animals safe.

5. Stay with your group at all times. Do not wander away on your own.

6. Throw trash in the garbage. Litter can harm both people and animals.

Field Trips

Aquarium rules are designed to protect the animals and allow all visitors to experience the wonder of aquatic life.

Aquariums 17

A History of Aquariums

The world's first known aquariums date back at least 4,500 years. Today, aquariums continue to attract people interested in aquatic animals and their habitats.

Goldfish are successfully kept in glass containers in England.

2500 BC

1000 BC

1700s AD

The Chinese become the first known people to **breed** fish. Carp are raised for food.

The ancient Sumerians, from what is now Iraq, keep fish in **artificial** ponds.

18 Field Trips

British scientist Philip Gosse establishes the first public aquarium at England's London Zoo.

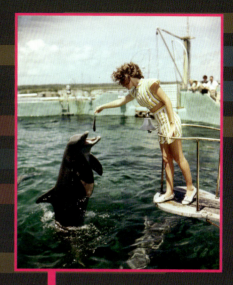

The world's first oceanarium opens in St. Augustine, Florida.

1853   **1856**   **1938**   **2018**

The Mote Marine Laboratory and Aquarium announces plans to build a new facility, at a cost of $130 million.

American businessman P. T. Barnum opens the first U.S. aquarium in New York City.

Aquariums | 19

Who Works at an Aquarium?

Aquariums require the knowledge and expertise of a variety of people. Some help take care of animals. Others participate in research and conservation programs.

Aquarists

Aquarists are the people who take care of the animals in an aquarium. They feed them and clean their tanks. Aquarists are also responsible for providing the animals with **enrichment** opportunities.

20 Field Trips

Curators

Curators decide on the animals that will be in each exhibit tank and how the tank will be set up. Curators also manage other workers in the aquarium.

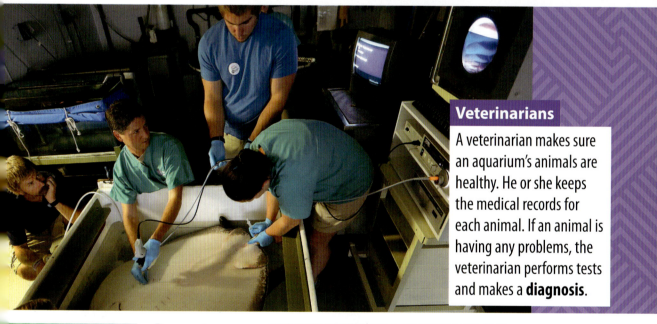

Veterinarians

A veterinarian makes sure an aquarium's animals are healthy. He or she keeps the medical records for each animal. If an animal is having any problems, the veterinarian performs tests and makes a **diagnosis**.

Marine Biologists

These scientists provide expert knowledge about the animals at the aquarium. They advise other staff on animal behavior and care. Marine biologists also work on conservation and research projects set up by the aquarium.

10 Questions to Test Your Knowledge

1. What can people learn about at an aquarium?
2. Which type of aquarium is a type of zoo?
3. Which aquarium is the largest in the United States?
4. What materials are most commonly used to create a tank's viewing area?
5. Which aquarium is working with medical scientists to fight cancer?
6. Who were the first known people to breed fish?
7. Why should people never bang on a fish tank?
8. Where was the world's first oceanarium established?
9. Who opened the first aquarium in the United States?
10. Which aquarium employees decide on the animals that go in each exhibit tank?

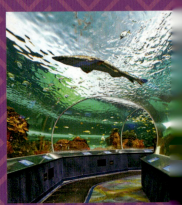

ANSWERS: 1. Aquatic life **2.** Public aquarium **3.** Georgia Aquarium **4.** Glass and acrylic **5.** Aquarium of the Pacific **6.** The Chinese **7.** It can scare the animals inside. **8.** St. Augustine, Florida **9.** P. T. Barnum **10.** Curators

22 Field Trips

Key Words

acrylic: a kind of plastic

aquatic: relating to water

artificial: produced by humans instead of by nature

breed: to keep animals for the purpose of producing offspring

conservation: the act of trying to keep an animal or plant from extinction

diagnosis: a judgment about what a particular illness or problem is after a medical exam

enrichment: the opportunity for animals to have a stimulating life and engage in natural behaviors

exhibit: public display

extinct: no longer existing

habitats: the natural environments of living things

laboratories: rooms designed for scientific experiments

marine: having to do with the ocean

native: a plant or animal that grows or lives naturally in a place

oceanarium: an aquarium that focuses on animals that live in the world's oceans

organisms: living things

photosynthesis: how plants make food

species: groups of animals with common characteristics

submarine: functioning or operating under water

Index

AquaRio 8
aquarists 20
Aquarium of the Pacific 12, 13, 22

Barnum, P. T. 19, 22

conservation aquariums 7
curators 21, 22

dolphinarium 6
dolphins 4, 6, 7

Georgia Aquarium 8, 22
Gosse, Philip 19

marine biologists 21
marine parks 7
Moscow Oceanarium 9
Mote Marine Laboratory and Aquarium 12, 19

National Aquarium 13

oceanarium 6, 9, 19, 22
orcas 7, 9

public aquariums 6, 19, 22

research 7, 12, 20, 21
research aquariums 7, 12

SEA LIFE Michigan Aquarium 13
SEA LIFE Sydney Aquarium 9
Shanghai Ocean Aquarium 9
sharks 8, 9

tanks 6, 8, 9, 10, 11, 15, 16, 20, 21, 22
tours 14, 15
tunnels 8, 9

uShaka Marine World 9

veterinarians 21

Aquariums 23

Get the best of both worlds.
AV2 bridges the gap between print and digital.

The expandable resources toolbar enables quick access to content including **videos**, **audio**, **activities**, **weblinks**, **slideshows**, **quizzes**, and **key words**.

Animated videos make static images come alive.

Resource icons on each page help readers to further **explore key concepts**.

Published by AV2
14 Penn Plaza 9th Floor
New York, NY 10122
Website: www.av2books.com

Copyright © 2021 AV2
All rights reserved. No part of this publication may be reproduced, stored in a retrieval system, or transmitted in any form or by any means, electronic, mechanical, photocopying, recording, or otherwise, without the prior written permission of the publisher.

Library of Congress Cataloging-in-Publication Data
Names: Reitmann, Kathleen, author. | Kissock, Heather, author.
Title: Aquariums / Kathleen Reitmann and Heather Kissock.
Description: New York, NY : AV2, 2021. | Series: Field trips | Includes index. | Audience: Grades 4-6
Identifiers: LCCN 2020010943 (print) | LCCN 2020010944 (ebook) | ISBN 9781791121471 (library binding) | ISBN 9781791121488 (paperback) | ISBN 9781791121495 | ISBN 9781791121501
Subjects: LCSH: Public aquariums--Juvenile literature.
Classification: LCC QL78 .R45 2021 (print) | LCC QL78 (ebook) | DDC 597.073--dc23
LC record available at https://lccn.loc.gov/2020010943
LC ebook record available at https://lccn.loc.gov/2020010944

Printed in Guangzhou, China
1 2 3 4 5 6 7 8 9 0   24 23 22 21 20

052020
101119

Editor: Heather Kissock
Designer: Terry Paulhus

Every reasonable effort has been made to trace ownership and to obtain permission to reprint copyright material. The publishers would be pleased to have any errors or omissions brought to their attention so that they may be corrected in subsequent printings.

AV2 acknowledges Getty Images, Alamy, iStock, Shutterstock, Wikimedia Commons, and the National Aquarium as its primary image suppliers for this title.